SOUTH AMERICA

by Madeline Donaldson

Lerner Publications Company • Minneapolis

Lerner Publications Company
A division of Lerner Publishing Group
241 First Avenue North
Minneapolis, MN 55401 USA

Website address: www.lernerbooks.com

Words in **bold type** are explained in a glossary on page 30.

Library of Congress Cataloging-in-Publication Data

Donaldson, Madeline.
    South America / by Madeline Donaldson.
       p.   cm. – (Pull ahead books)
    Summary: An introduction to the geography, plants and animals, and people of the continent of South America.
Includes bibliographical references and index.
     ISBN-13: 978–0–8225–4723–5 (lib. bdg. : alk. paper)
     ISBN-10: 0–8225–4723–6 (lib. bdg. : alk. paper)
     1. South America–Juvenile literature. [1. South
America.] I. Title. II. Series.
F2208.5.D66 2005
980–dc22   2003019974

Manufactured in the United States of America
2 3 4 5 6 7 – JR – 12 11 10 09 08 07

Photographs are used with the permission of: © Robert Francis/South American Pictures, p. 3; © Cory Langley, p. 6; © Tony Morrison/South American Pictures, pp. 7, 9, 10–11, 12, 14–15, 16, 18, 20, 24–25, 26–27; © Ricardo Funari/RF2/Latin Focus.com, pp. 8, © Alex Ocampo/ LatinFocus.com, 19, 22–23; © Kathy Jarvis/South American Pictures, p. 13; Photo by Dr. Roma Hoff, p. 17; © John Kreul/Independent Picture Service, p. 21. Maps on pp. 4–5 and 29 by Laura Westlund.

Where could you hear birds screech in the world's largest **tropical rain forest?**

The **continent** of South America!

Arctic Ocean

North America

Atlantic Ocean

Pacific Ocean

South America

Antarctica

A continent is a big piece of land.
There are seven continents on Earth.

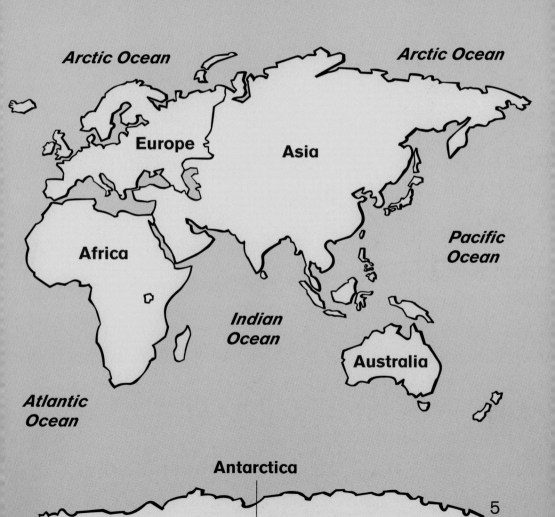

Arctic Ocean

Arctic Ocean

Europe

Asia

Africa

Pacific
Ocean

Indian
Ocean

Australia

Atlantic
Ocean

Antarctica

Whoosh! Oceans lie on either side of South America.

The **coastlines** of South America are long! South Americans enjoy the sandy beaches along the coasts.

South America has many rivers. The continent's longest river is the Amazon.

Waterfalls crash over cliffs into some rivers. Angel Falls drops a long way down into the Churún River.

Do you remember the largest rain forest?
It is called the Amazon Rain Forest.

South America also has mountains, grasslands, and deserts.

The Andes Mountains stretch in a long line from northern South America to southern South America.

Baa! Baa! Farmers raise animals and crops in small areas near the Andes.

Wide grasslands cover much of South America. The grasslands in the south are called the **pampas.**

Mooo! Large **herds** of cattle eat the grasses of the pampas.

The Atacama Desert is the driest place
in South America. The Atacama gets
almost no rain.

South America is home to lots of different kinds of animals. These llamas live in the Andes.

A toucan sits on
a branch in South
America's rain
forest.

Penguins make their homes in the far south of South America.

Flowers and trees grow well in South America. The wood of the balsa tree is strong and light. It is easy to carry.

Mmmm! Beautiful tropical orchids give off a sweet smell.

South America has twelve **countries.**
The continent also has one **territory**
that isn't a country.

More than 350 million people live in South America. Most South Americans live in cities.

This is the city of Buenos Aires in the country of Argentina.

Brazil is the continent's largest country. It covers most of northeastern South America.

This is the city of Rio de Janeiro in eastern Brazil.

South America has many interesting places!
Do you know about Machu Picchu?

It is an old city in the Andes built by
people called the **Incas.**

There's always
something new
to learn about
South America!

Cool Facts about South America

- South America covers almost 700 million square miles (1.8 million square kilometers).

- The main rivers of South America are the Amazon River, the Madeira River, the Orinoco River, the Magdalena River, and the Paraná River.

- The animals of South America include anteaters, armadillos, egrets, rheas, sloths, and tapirs.

- The plants of South America include mahogany and balsa trees, sisal plants, and coca shrubs.

- Most South Americans speak Spanish, Portuguese, or local languages.

- The large cities of South America include Rio de Janeiro, São Paulo, Bogotá, and Buenos Aires.

Map of South America

Glossary

coastlines: the shores, or edges, of land that are touched by the ocean

continent: one of seven big pieces of land on Earth

countries: places with their own government and borders (or edges)

herds: large groups of the same kind of animals

Incas: a group of people who lived in western South America about 600 years ago

pampas: the grassy plains of southern South America

territory: an area that is ruled by another country

tropical rain forest: a rich, green forest that gets a lot of rain throughout the year

Further Reading and Websites

Dell'Oro, Suzanne Paul. *Argentina.* Minneapolis: Carolrhoda Books, Inc., 1998.

Fowler, Allan. *South America.* Danbury, CT: Children's Press, 2001.

Fox, Mary Virginia. *South America.* Crystal Lake, IL: Heinemann Library, 2002.

Haskins, Jim, and Kathleen Benson. *Count Your Way through Brazil.* Minneapolis: Carolrhoda Books, Inc., 1996.

Jones, Helga. *Venezuela.* Minneapolis: Carolrhoda Books, Inc., 2000.

Nelson, Robin. *Where Is My Continent?* Minneapolis: Lerner Publications Company, 2002.

Sayre, April Pulley. *South America, Surprise!* Brookfield, CT: Millbrook, 2003.

Weitzman, Elizabeth. *Brazil.* Minneapolis: Carolrhoda Books, Inc., 1998.

Enchanted Learning
http://enchantedlearning.com
Search the geography section of this website to find links to South America.

Enchanted Learning: All about Rain Forests
http://enchantedlearning.com/subjects/rainforest/
This site has lots of information on the animals, soil, plants, and people of the rain forests.

Index